Collins
INTERNATIONAL

T0337523

Science Foundation
Activity Book C

Published by Collins
An imprint of HarperCollins*Publishers*
The News Building, 1 London Bridge Street,
London, SE1 9GF, UK

HarperCollins Publishers
Macken House, 39/40 Mayor Street Upper,
Dublin 1, D01 C9W8, Ireland

Browse the complete Collins catalogue at
www.collins.co.uk

© HarperCollins*Publishers* Limited 2021

10 9 8 7 6

ISBN 978-0-00-846872-9

British Library Cataloguing-in-Publication Data
A catalogue record for this publication is available from the British Library.

Author: Fiona Macgregor
Publisher: Elaine Higgleton
Product manager: Letitia Luff
Commissioning editor: Rachel Houghton
Edited by: Eleanor Barber
Editorial management: Oriel Square
Cover designer: Kevin Robbins
Cover illustrations: Jouve India Pvt Ltd.
Internal illustrations: Jouve India Pvt. Ltd.;
p 5, p17 Tasneem Amiruddin, p 22c1 Jon Stuart
Typesetter: Jouve India Pvt. Ltd.
Production controller: Lyndsey Rogers

Printed in India by Multivista Global Pvt. Ltd.

Acknowledgements

With thanks to all the kindergarten staff and their schools around the world who
have helped with the development of this course, by sharing insights and
commenting on and testing sample materials:

Calcutta International School: Sharmila Majumdar, Mrs Pratima Nayar, Preeti
Roychoudhury, Tinku Yadav, Lakshmi Khanna, Mousumi Guha, Radhika Dhanuka,
Archana Tiwari, Urmita Das; Gateway College (Sri Lanka): Kousala Benedict; Hawar
International School: Kareen Barakat, Shahla Mohammed, Jennah Hussain; Manthan
International School: Shalini Reddy; Monterey Pre-Primary: Adina Oram; Prometheus
School: Aneesha Sahni, Deepa Nanda; Pragyanam School: Monika Sachdev; Rosary
Sisters High School: Samar Sabat, Sireen Freij, Hiba Mousa; Solitaire Global School:
Devi Nimmagadda; United Charter Schools (UCS): Tabassum Murtaza; Vietnam
Australia International School: Holly Simpson

The publishers wish to thank the following for permission to reproduce photographs.

(t = top, c = centre, b = bottom, r = right, l = left)

p 18tl OBprod/Shutterstock, p 18tr Sanit Ratsameephot/Shutterstock, p 18bl
A3pfamily/Shutterstock, p 18br New Africa/Shutterstock, p 20t chittakorn59/
Shutterstock, p 20c1 Namning/Shutterstock, p 20c2 Brian A Jackson/Shutterstock,
p 20c3 Quang Ho/Shutterstock, p 20c4 Ascannio/Shutterstock, p 20b Mega Pixel/
Shutterstock, p 22t Maksim Chaikou/Shutterstock, p 22c2 Mark Coote, p 22b
OBprod/Shutterstock

Extracts from Collins Big Cat readers reprinted by permission of HarperCollins
Publishers Ltd

All © HarperCollins*Publishers*

MIX
Paper | Supporting
responsible forestry
FSC™ C007454

This book contains FSC™ certified paper and other controlled
sources to ensure responsible forest management.

For more information visit: www.harpercollins.co.uk/green

Draw and say

Which weather do you like or not like?
Draw 😊 or 🙁.   Date:

Find and say

Find five differences between the pictures of a warm dry day and a cold wet day.

Date:

Follow

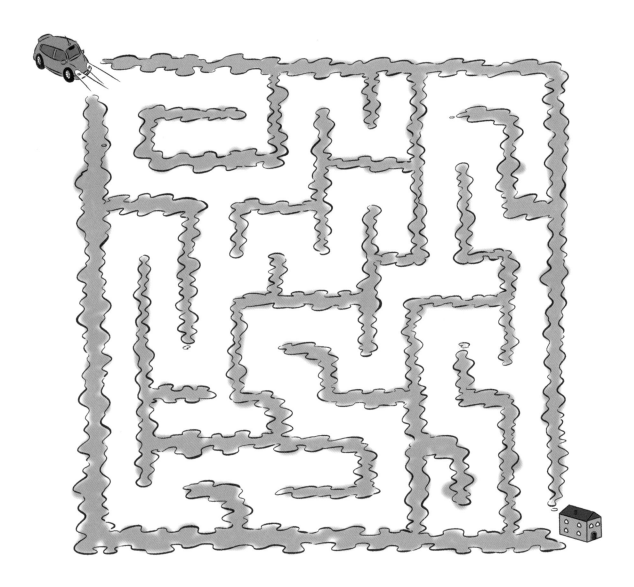

Fog is thick cloud that makes it difficult to see things.
Help the car get safely through the fog.
Find the way home.

Date:

Match and say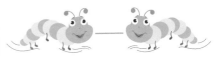

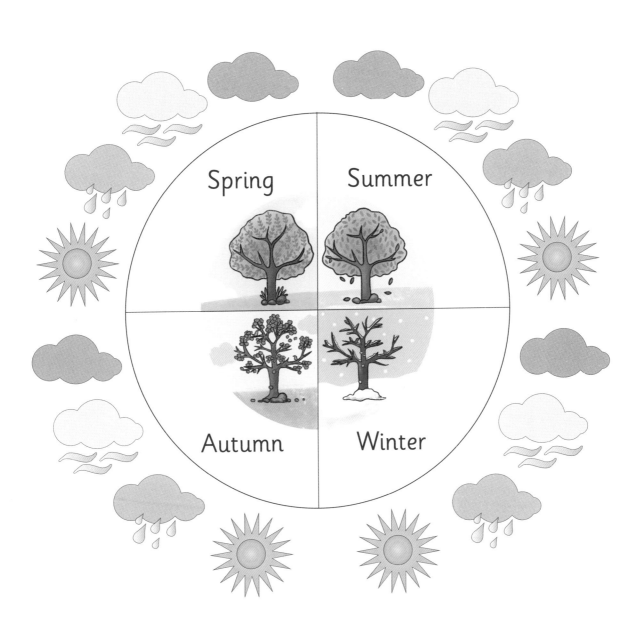

Match the kinds of weather to the seasons in your country.

Date:

Sort

metal

fabric

wood

stone

wood

stone

metal

fabric

PCM 17. Cut out the pictures.
Stick them in the correct place.

Date:

Tick

Object	Tick when found
pencil	
table	
spoon	
paper	
card	
book	

These objects are made of wood.
Are they made of wood in your classroom?
Put a tick next to the wooden objects you find.   Date:

Circle and say

Circle the things made of wood.
What other materials can you see?   Date:

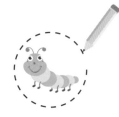

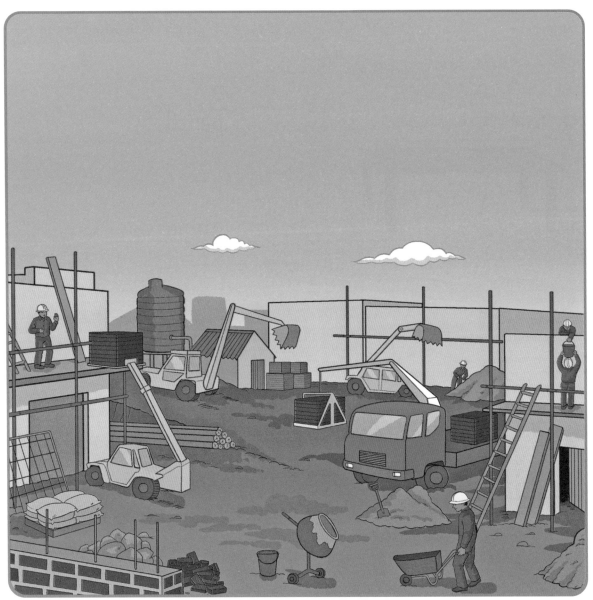

Date:

Circle and say

Which things are made of metal?
Circle them. Say what they are.

Date:

Circle and count

Find and circle the litter.
How many pieces of litter did you find?   Date:

Sort

Food

Paper

Plastic

Metal

PCM 18. Cut up the pictures. Sort the litter.
Stick it in the correct bin.

Date:

Circle and say

Where is water being wasted in this picture?
Circle and say.

Date:

Make a plan

What can you do to save water? Draw your ideas.

Date:

Draw

Toys that work by pushing

Draw a picture of yourself pushing a toy.

Date:

Tick and say

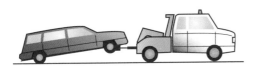 ☐

 ☐

 ☐

 ☐

 ☐

 ☐

Tick the pictures that show a pulling action.

Date:

Sort

Push	Pull

PCM 19. Cut up the pictures.
Stick the pushing actions in the purple box.
Stick the pulling actions in the yellow box.

Date:

Draw

Draw an arrow under each picture to show in
which direction the object will move.   Date:

Can you?

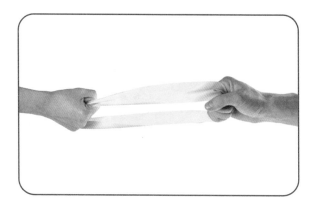

stretch ☐

bend ☐

twist ☐

squash ☐

Do the actions. Ask a friend to tick the boxes
to show you did the actions.   Date:

Draw

Draw an arrow under each picture to show in
which direction the object will move.   Date:

Can you?

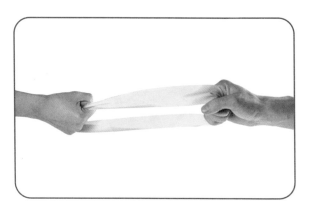

stretch ☐

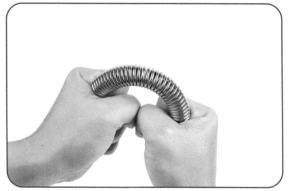

bend ☐

twist ☐

squash ☐

Do the actions. Ask a friend to tick the boxes
to show you did the actions.   Date:

Do this

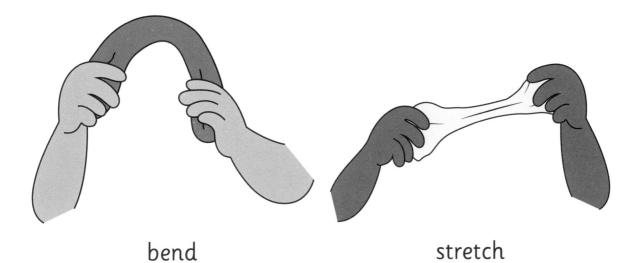

bend   stretch

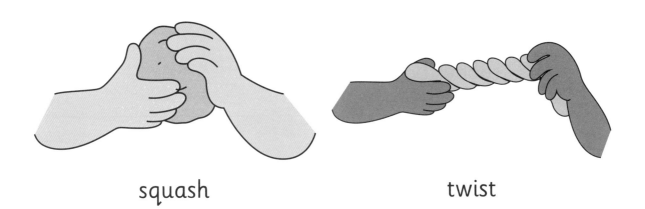

squash   twist

Use your modelling clay to do
the actions in the pictures.

Date:

Tick

	bend	stretch
stone		
sponge		
modelling clay		
rubber band		
sticky tack		
ball		

Try the actions with the different materials.
Tick the boxes if you can do the action.   Date:

Colour and tick

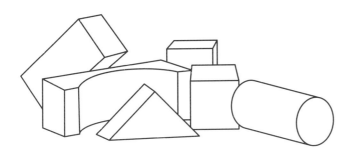

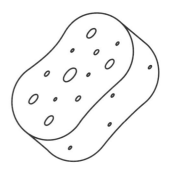

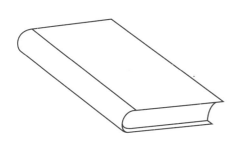

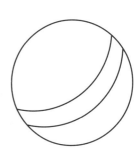

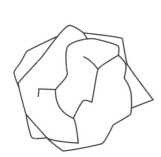

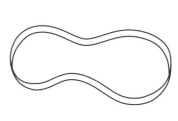

Colour the things that twist.
Tick the things that squash.

Date:

Revie

Match

It can stretch.

It is raining.

Pick up the litter.

She is pulling.

Match the sentences to the pictures.　　　Date:

Review

Tick

☐ I can draw and say.

☐ I can find and say.

☐ I can match.

☐ I can sort.

☐ I can tick.

☐ I can circle and say.

☐ I can circle and count.

☐ I can look.

☐ I can colour.

Tick what you can do.	Date:

Assessment record

_____ has achieved these Science Foundation Phase Objectives:

Describe daily weather	1	2	3
Understand that weather changes from day to day	1	2	3
Connect clothing and activities to hot and cold weather	1	2	3
Describe objects in terms of the materials used to make them	1	2	3
Identify and name common materials	1	2	3
Understand that litter is waste disposed of incorrectly	1	2	3
Understand that water is a resource that needs saving	1	2	3
Identify personal actions needed to save water	1	2	3
Explore and describe how pushes and pulls move things	1	2	3
Investigate how to change movement using pushes and pulls	1	2	3
Explore how actions change the shape of some materials	1	2	3

1: Partially achieved
2: Achieved
3: Exceeded

Signed by teacher:
Signed by parent: Date: